Usborne

Festivals!

Written by JANE BINGHAM

Illustrated by MARIONA CABASSA

Designed by FRANKIE ALLEN

Edited by FELICITY BROOKS

With expert advice from Amy Chiu, Gade Gray, Stella Satapon Gray, Sahrish Nadim, John Partington, Yoshiho Pryer, Sreya Rao, and Daniel Susskind.

CONTENTS

This book is filled with festivals from around the world. Some celebrate an important day for a religion. Some welcome a season of the year. Some are held in memory of a special person – and some are simply about having a good time.

SPLAT!

These fun-filled celebrations are all about throwing things.

Squishy tomatoes whizz through the air at the Spanish festival of **La Tomatina**.

Everyone gets smothered in paint at the Indian festival of **Holi**.

Holi is often known as the Spring Festival.

After the festival, the streets are hosed down with water.

People throw rubber boots on **Gumboot Day** in New Zealand.

BOO!

Sometimes it's fun to feel a little frightened. Check out these spooky festivals if you dare!

TRICK or TREAT?

WOOOOO!

We go 'trick-or-treating' in scary costumes.

People used to believe that ghosts visited the Earth at **Halloween** and made trouble if they weren't given treats.

This carved pumpkin is called a jack-o'-lantern.

Everyone dresses up on the **Day of the Dead** in Mexico.

Streets and houses are decorated with paper banners.

It's a joyful time when we remember our loved ones.

We sing and dance for our ancestors.

Festima celebrates traditional dancing masks from West Africa.

The dancers look really fierce.

Masks have been worn at the **Venice Carnival** since the Middle Ages.

Some masks are quite sinister.

Food and flowers are laid out on altars.

Pets are remembered too.

SPLOSH!

Everyone gets wet and messy at these festivals.

In Thailand, people welcome the New Year with a water festival called **Songkran**.

Some people bathe statues of the Buddha at Songkran.

Teams race through the rapids at the **Zambezi White Water Festival** in Zambia.

Everyone sploshes around in mud at the **Boryeong Mud Festival** in South Korea.

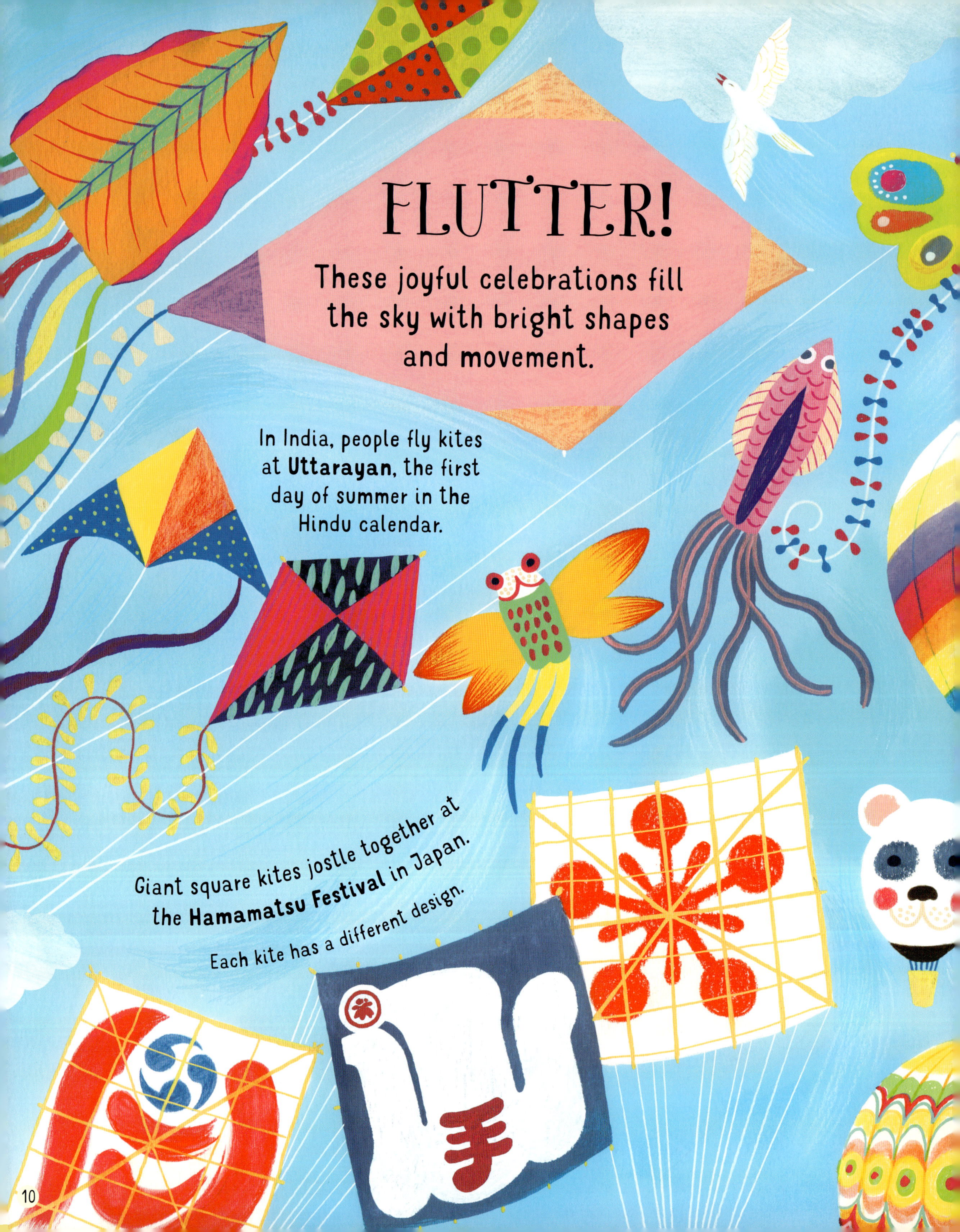

FLUTTER!

These joyful celebrations fill the sky with bright shapes and movement.

In India, people fly kites at **Uttarayan**, the first day of summer in the Hindu calendar.

Giant square kites jostle together at the **Hamamatsu Festival** in Japan.

Each kite has a different design.

The festival of **Kodomo no Hi** celebrates the chidren of Japan.

Fish-shaped banners represent everyone in the family.

Many countries hold **hot-air balloon festivals**.

Some of the balloons are amazing shapes.

People enjoy the beauty of cherry tree blossom at the Japanese festival of **Hanami**.

GLOW!

All these festivals feature candles as symbols of hope.

Diwali is a five-day festival of lights.

Hindus, Sikhs and Jains all celebrate Diwali.

At **Hanukkah**, Jewish people light candles in a candle-holder called a menorah.

Each evening, they light one more candle.

Hanukkah lasts for eight days.

On **Saint Lucia's Day**, Swedish children wear white robes and carry candles and wands.

In the past, the candles had real flames.

People send paper lanterns floating into the sky at the **Yi Peng Festival** in Thailand.

They let the past drift away with the lanterns.

Another Thai festival is **Loy Krathong**. People float lamps on canals, rivers and lakes.

The lamps are made from banana stems and leaves, and decorated with flowers and incense sticks.

CRACKLE!

Fire and fireworks light up the sky at these dramatic celebrations.

The **Burning of Zozobra** marks the end of summer in Santa Fe, USA.

Zozobra is also known as Old Man Gloom.

We write down our worries and put them in a Gloom Box.

The box is burned with Zozobra.

People let off fireworks on **Guy Fawkes Night** in Britain.

Sometimes they set fire to a model of Guy Fawkes, the man who plotted to blow up Parliament.

German legends say that witches visit the Earth on **Walpurgis Night.**

Everyone makes loud noises to frighten the witches away.

WoO!

Every year, the grassy top of Japan's **Mount Wakakusa** is set on fire.

Huge crowds gather to watch the mountain burn.

All over the world, people welcome the **New Year** with spectacular firework displays.

The Scottish festival of **Up Helly Aa** has a Viking theme.

At the end of the festival, a Viking longship is set on fire.

SPARKLE!

The sparkle of ice and snow adds a wintry magic to these festivals.

Canada's **Carnaval de Québec** is a huge midwinter festival.

There are night parades led by giant angels, ice-skating contests, and a canoe race on the river.

Christmas is a Christian festival to celebrate Christ's birth.

At Christmas, children open presents delivered by Santa Claus.

The world's biggest **ice festival** is held at **Harbin**, in China.

Everyone marvels at the massive icy castles.

DANCE!

All around the world, people celebrate the joy of music and dance.

'Whirling dervishes' perform graceful dances at the **Rumi festival** in Turkey.

The dancers keep whirling until they are in a trance.

Huge crowds of people dance to the music at **music festivals**.

WOMAD festivals celebrate world music, arts and dance. They are held in many countries.

Spring is welcomed with **May Day** dancing in some British villages.

Children dance around a maypole.

Once a year, Indigenous Americans come together for the **Gathering of Nations** at Albuquerque, New Mexico.

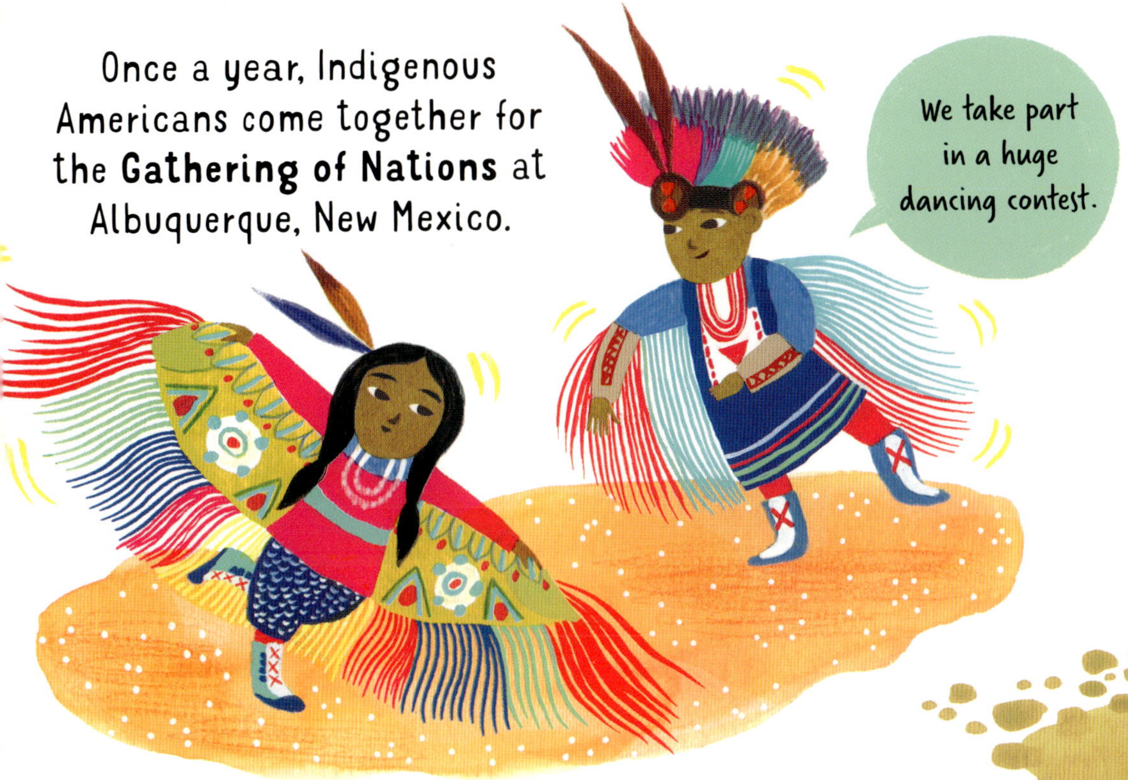

Aboriginal Australians demonstrate their traditional dances at the **Barunga Festival.**

People perform Bhangra folk dances at the Sikh festival of **Vaisakhi**.

At Vaisakhi, Sikhs remember how their religion began.

The Lion Dance is part of the celebrations for **Chinese New Year**.

Two dancers hide inside the lion costume.

Often, the lions dance on tall platforms.

FEAST!

People get together at festival times to enjoy special meals and traditional foods.

The festival of **Eid al-Fitr** marks the end of Ramadan, the Muslim holy month of fasting.

Muslims gather for a feast.

Some families eat ma'amoul – a kind of cookie filled with figs, dates and nuts.

People hold a **Monkey Buffet** at the Lopburi temples in Thailand.

The Christian festival of **Easter** has become an international celebration.

Children hunt for chocolate eggs on Easter Day.

Mexicans eat cookies shaped like skulls on the **Day of the Dead.**

At **Thanksgiving,** American families eat roast turkey...

...and pumpkin pie.

They remember the first harvest feast of the early settlers in North America.

Rosh Hashanah marks the start of the Jewish New Year.

Apples dipped in honey symbolize a sweet new year ahead.

The fish represents many blessings.

Mince pies, Christmas pudding and gingerbread are popular **Christmas** treats.

Sometimes, the pudding has silver coins hidden inside it.

They offer food to the monkeys that live in the temple ruins.

RACE!

These festivals will get your pulse racing – whether you're taking part or just watching the fun.

Some English villages hold a **Pancake Day Race**.

The **Palio** is held twice a year in the Italian city of Siena.

Ten horses with bareback riders represent the city's districts.

The boat race is the highlight of China's **Dragon Boat Festival**.

The Woolly Worm Festival is held in North Carolina, USA. Caterpillars race up strings and the winner is the first to reach the top.

A drum is thumped to set the pace for the crew.

PARADE!

People of all ages love to join in the fun of a big parade.

The Parade of Giants is one of the highlights of the Spanish festival of **La Mercè**.

Saint Patrick is the patron saint of Ireland.

Irish people celebrate **Saint Patrick's Day** with a lively parade.

The **Désalpes Festival** in Switzerland is a parade of cows!

At the end of summer, the cows parade down the mountain to their winter fields.

A giant dragon leads the parade to welcome the **Chinese New Year**.

The dance team uses long poles to make the dragon twist and turn.

Many cities hold carnival parades for **Mardi Gras**.

LOOK AGAIN!

Can you find your way through the wonderful world of festivals? Try the challenges on these pages.

Where can you spot a pair of lanterns like these?

Can you name the festival this spooky pair are enjoying?

Which religious festival is celebrated by eating these foods?

What is this dancing lion celebrating?

What fiery celebration are these children taking part in?

Where in the book is this hot-air balloon?

How many other hot-air balloons can you find?

What do these fish represent?

Do you know the name of this messy festival?

Can you name the event this crew is taking part in?

Answers on page 30.

More about festivals

Over the next five pages, you can find out more about the festivals shown in this book.

SPLAT! pages 4–5

La Tomatina

When? Last Wednesday in August
Where? Buñol, Spain
What? People throw squishy tomatoes at each other.
Why? A quarrel in 1945 became an annual event.

Holi

When? 2 days in February or March
Where? India
What? Hindus throw grains onto bonfires and smear each other with water and powdered paint.
Why? To celebrate the coming of spring.

Gumboot Day

When? March or April
Where? Taihape, New Zealand
What? Competitions to see who can throw a boot the furthest and for the 'best dressed gumboot'.
Why? To celebrate rubber Wellington boots.

BOO! pages 6–7

Halloween

When? 31 October
Where? USA and many other countries
What? People dress up in scary costumes and offer neighbours a trick or treat.
Why? People believed dead souls returned on this night and played tricks if they weren't given treats.

Festima

When? February or March, every 2 years
Where? Dédougou, Burkina Faso
What? People perform traditional dances wearing enormous masks and elaborate costumes.
Why? To celebrate African masks and mask-makers.

Day of the Dead

When? 1–2 November
Where? Mexico and Mexican communities
What? People dress up as skeletons, join parades to greet dead souls, and leave gifts at family graves.
Why? People believed the souls of the dead returned on All Souls Night (The Day of the Dead).

Venice Carnival

When? February or March
Where? Venice, Italy
What? Processions, grand costume balls. Famous for elaborate masks, with a competition for the best.
Why? Originally to celebrate a military victory in 1162.

SPLOSH! pages 8–9

Songkran

When? 13–15 April
Where? Thailand
What? People splash water on each other to wash away bad luck and welcome new blessings.
Why? Marks Thailand's traditional New Year.

Zambezi White Water Festival

When? October
Where? Livingstone, Zambia
What? Crews race boats through the rapids, and cheering crowds enjoy food, music and dancing.
Why? To celebrate Zambezi River's wild waters below Mosi-oa-Tunya (also known as Victoria Falls).

Boryeong Mud Festival

When? 2 weeks in July or August
Where? Boryeong, South Korea
What? Activities include a mud pool, mud slides and mud skiing. Cosmetics made from the mud are sold.
Why? To celebrate Boryeong's muddy beaches.

FLUTTER! pages 10–11

Uttarayan

When? 14–15 January
Where? Gujarat state, India
What? Hindus fly kites of paper and bamboo. At night, kites filled with lights and candles are flown.
Why? To celebrate summer's start and winter's end.

Hamamatsu Festival

When? 3–5 May
Where? Hamamatsu, Japan
What? Kite-flying. Includes 'quarrel kite' battles when pilots coil their strings around others' to snap them.
Why? Dates to the 1560s when people of the city flew kites to welcome the baby son of a local lord.

Albuquerque International Balloon Fiesta

When? 1st full week in October, for 9 days
Where? Albuquerque, New Mexico, USA
What? Balloon festival. Includes a 'special shape rodeo' and a 'dawn patrol' that begins in darkness.
Why? To celebrate and enjoy hot-air ballooning.

Kodomo no Hi

When? 5 May
Where? Japan
What? Families fly windsocks in the shape of carp. Each fish represents a different family member.
Why? To celebrate children.

Hanami

When? End of March to beginning of May
Where? Japan and Japanese communities
What? Picnics among the blossoming cherry trees.
Why? To celebrate the beauty of the blossoming trees and the coming of spring.

GLOW! pages 12–13

Diwali

When? 5 days in October or November
Where? India and Indian communities
What? Feasts, fireworks. People light lamps called 'diyas' and draw rangoli patterns outside their homes.
Why? To celebrate the triumph of good over evil.

Hanukkah

When? 8 days and nights in November or December
Where? Jewish communities worldwide
What? Special food, games with a 'dreidel' (spinning top). People exchange gifts and light candles on a candlestick with 9 branches called a 'menorah'.
Why? To remember when the Jews recaptured Jerusalem and rededicated their holy temple.

Saint Lucia's Day

When? December
Where? Sweden, Norway and Finland
What? Children wear white robes in a procession. Boys carry wands, girls wear 'candle crowns'.
Why? To honour Saint Lucia, patron saint of light.

Yi Peng

When? November
Where? Northern Thailand
What? People launch lanterns of bamboo and tissue paper into the sky on the night of a full moon.
Why? People write wishes on the lanterns. Watching until one disappears is believed to bring good luck.

Loy Krathong

When? November
Where? Thailand
What? People make 'krathongs' (lotus-shaped baskets decorated with flowers, incense sticks and a candle) and float them on lakes and rivers.
Why? To give thanks to the goddess of water.

CRACKLE! pages 14–15

Burning of Zozobra
When? Early September
Where? Santa Fe, New Mexico, USA
What? A giant wooden figure of Zozobra, or 'Old Man Gloom', is burnt on top of a bonfire.
Why? To clear away all the gloom and troubles of the past year and bring in a new, better one.

Mount Wakakusa Fire Festival
When? 4th Saturday of January
Where? Mount Wakakusa, near Nara, Japan
What? Buddhist and Shinto priests burn the long grass on the hilltop and people let off fireworks.
Why? Recalls the 1760 burning of Mount Wakakusa.

New Year's Eve *(called Hogmanay in Scotland)*
When? 31 December
Where? Worldwide
What? Fireworks. In English-speaking countries, people link arms to sing 'Auld Lang Syne'. In Scotland, people visit friends' houses with a drink and a lump of coal (called 'first footing').
Why? To welcome the New Year.

Guy Fawkes Night *(also called Bonfire Night)*
When? 5 November
Where? UK
What? Fireworks. People burn a 'guy' (a dummy of old clothes stuffed with straw) on a bonfire.
Why? Remembers 1605 'Gunpowder Plot' when Guy Fawkes tried to blow up the Houses of Parliament.

Walpurgis Night
When? 30 April
Where? Germany; northern and central Europe
What? People light bonfires, sing songs and make loud noises to scare away witches.
Why? In honour of Saint Walpurga, believed to protect people from witchcraft.

Up Helly Aa
When? January, February or March
Where? Shetland Islands, Scotland
What? In Lerwick, the biggest festival, an imitation Viking longship is burnt after a torchlit procession.
Why? Marks the end of Yule (Christmas) season.

SPARKLE! pages 16–17

Carnaval de Québec
When? February onwards
Where? Québec, Canada
What? Bonhomme, a giant snowman, leads parades. Snowboarding, ice canoeing and sledding contests.
Why? To celebrate the beauty of late winter.

Christmas
When? 24–25 December (Eastern Orthodox Christians celebrate on 7 January.)
Where? Worldwide
What? Christians sing carols in church. People feast, decorate Christmas trees and give gifts. Children hang stockings for Santa Claus to fill with presents.
Why? To celebrate Jesus Christ's birth.

Harbin International Ice and Snow Festival
When? January to February
Where? Harbin, Northern China
What? Includes snow sculptures and full-size buildings made from ice from the Songhua River.
Why? To celebrate the beauty of snow and ice.

DANCE! pages 18–19

Rumi Whirling Dervishes Festival
When? 7–17 December
Where? Konya, Turkey
What? Dances by Rumi's followers, known as 'whirling dervishes'. These are a form of meditation.
Why? In honour of the great Muslim poet, Rumi.

Answers to the LOOK AGAIN! puzzles on pages 26–27

1. p. 12 (Diwali); 2. Halloween (p. 6); 3. Rosh Hashanah (p. 21); 4. The Burning of Zozobra (p. 14); 5. A Gloom Box (p. 14); 6. Chinese New Year (p. 19); 7. p. 11 (Hot-air balloon festivals); 8. 11 hot-air balloons altogether; 9. Each fish represents a family member (p. 11); 10. Holi (p. 4–5); 11. Zambezi White Water Festival (p. 8–9)

WOMAD Festival

When? Throughout the year
Where? Various locations, including Australia, UK, Abu Dhabi, Italy, Spain and Chile
What? A music, arts and dance festival.
Why? To represent music, art and dance worldwide.

May Day

When? 1 May
Where? Villages and towns in the UK and Europe
What? Traditionally includes dancing around a maypole and crowning a Queen of the May.
Why? To welcome spring.

Gathering of Nations

When? 4th weekend in April
Where? Albuquerque, New Mexico, USA
What? Indigenous Americans from over 700 tribes gather. Dancing, singing and drumming competitions.
Why? To celebrate Indigenous American culture.

Barunga Festival

When? 3 days in early June
Where? Barunga, Northern Territory, Australia
What? Indigenous Australian dance, music, sports and art. Didgeridoo competition and story-telling.
Why? Celebrates Indigenous Australian culture.

Vaisakhi

When? 13 or 14 April
Where? India and Sikh communities
What? Fairs, processions, dancing. Sikhs remember important events in the founding of their religion.
Why? To celebrate the spring harvest.

Chinese New Year

When? 15 days in January–February
Where? China and Chinese communities
What? Feasts, fireworks, parades. A Dragon Dance Parade and Lion Dance are said to bring good luck.
Why? Celebrates New Year in the Chinese calendar.

FEAST! pages 20–21

Eid al-Fitr

When? Date follows the Islamic calendar
Where? Muslim communities worldwide
What? People attend religious services, join in processions, decorate their homes, and feast.
Why? End of Ramadan (the Muslim month of fasting).

Easter

When? March or April
Where? Worldwide
What? Christians sing special hymns in church. People give each other chocolate Easter eggs and children hunt for eggs hidden by the Easter Bunny.
Why? To celebrate the resurrection (rising) of Jesus Christ from the dead.

Monkey Buffet Festival

When? Last Sunday of November
Where? Lopburi, Thailand
What? A feast is offered to the macaque monkeys that live among the temple ruins at Lopburi.
Why? In honour of the Hindu monkey god, Lord Hanuman, believed to have helped build the temples.

Rosh Hashanah

When? 2 days in September or October
Where? Jewish communities worldwide
What? People feast, attend services in synagogues, and listen to the blowing of a 'shofar' (a long, curved ram's horn that makes a very loud noise).
Why? Marks the start of the Jewish New Year.

Thanksgiving

When? 4th Thursday in November (USA) or 2nd Monday in October (Canada)
Where? USA and US communities; Canada
What? Family and friends feast and give thanks for the blessings of the past year.
Why? To remember a harvest feast held by early settlers in North America.

RACE! pages 22–23

Pancake Day *(also called Shrove Tuesday)*

When? February or March
Where? UK and worldwide
What? People eat pancakes. Some have pancake races, tossing their pancakes in a pan as they run.
Why? In the past, Christians cooked pancakes to use up spare ingredients before fasting in Lent.

Woolly Worm Festival

When? October
Where? Banner Elk, North Carolina, USA
What? 'Woolly worm' caterpillars race up strings. Their markings are said to predict the weather so the winner becomes the area's weather forecaster.
Why? Celebrates caterpillar of the Isabella tiger moth.

Palio di Siena

When? 2 July and 16 August
Where? Siena, Italy
What? 10 horses with bareback riders race 3 times around a track in front of the town hall.
Why? For entertainment. The riders represent 10 of the city's 17 districts.

Dragon Boat Festival

When? May or June
Where? China and Chinese communities
What? Boat races along rivers. People eat 'zongzi' (sticky rice dumplings) and throw some in the water.
Why? Remembers the search for Qu Yuan, a great Chinese poet who drowned in a river. People threw zongzi in the river to keep fish and evil spirits away.

PARADE! pages 24–25

La Mercè

When? 21–24 September
Where? Barcelona, Spain
What? Dancing, circus acts and creation of 'human towers'. Huge papier-mâché figures of kings, queens and nobles are paraded through the streets.
Why? To celebrate the city of Barcelona.

Saint Patrick's Day

When? 17 March
Where? Ireland and Irish communities
What? People wear green clothes, join a parade, and march, sing and dance.
Why? To honour Saint Patrick, who is the patron saint of Ireland.

Désalpes

When? End of September
Where? Villages in Switzerland
What? A parade of cows, wearing huge bells and flower garlands, led by farmers in national dress.
Why? To move cows from summer pastures in the high mountains to winter fields on the lower slopes.

Mardi Gras *(also called Carnival)*

When? February or March
Where? Cities across the world
What? Parades, dancing, feasting. Its name means 'Fat Tuesday'. The biggest carnivals are in New Orleans (USA) and Rio de Janeiro (Brazil).
Why? To feast and have fun before Lent.

Usborne Quicklinks

Visit Usborne Quicklinks for links to websites where you can watch people around the world celebrate their favourite festivals, from throwing tomatoes or powdered paints to parading in costumes, flying kites, making floating lamps and much more. **Go to usborne.com/Quicklinks** and type in the title of this book. Children should be supervised online. Please read our internet safety guidelines at Usborne Quicklinks.